PRIMITIVE

PRIMITIVE

GIL ADAMSON

To David,

most folks would sign
"best wishes", but me...

Bust wretches!

love Gil
Dec 1991

COACH HOUSE PRESS • TORONTO

Published with the assistance of the Canada
Council and the Ontario Arts Council

The author wishes to thank the Ontario Arts
Council for financial assistance. Some of these
poems have appeared previously in *Caliban* and
Mental Radio. Some titles were randomly
generated and so thanks to Jean Yoon and Kevin
Connolly for help and support.

Canadian Cataloguing in Publication

Adamson, Gil 1961 -
Primitive

Poems.
ISBN 0-88910-405-0

I. Title.

PS 8551.D35P7 1991   C811'.54   C91-094930-1
PR9199.3.A33P7 1991

CONTENTS

To my family

A gas station explodes
and for blocks
it looks like daylight.
The parking lot sinks in
the pumps shooting flame
candy wrappers floating down
like leaflets from a plane.
I am upset
but you think it's fun.
We drive back and forth looking.
Every time you touch me
the dashboard dims
and this worries me too.
I rub my thighs
thinking of what I should do.
We scream down the main street
turn and scream back.
You pull my skirt up
and bend down as I drive.
I imagine an accident
two tires bouncing
into the trees.

We wander into someone's yard.
There has been a party and
people sleep naked by the pool.
Empty chip bags blow over the lawn.
I run my fingers
through my hair and watch
as you slip out of your clothes.
I stare and you smile
when a dog bursts from the woods.
A black dog, mostly mouth.
It clears the fence, the deck chairs
tears the screen door like a missile.
Inside the house the lights go out.
Soon it is quiet again.
You get into the pool and float.

The water is bright blue
and eight lights shine around you.
I feel bad about all this
wonder if I should do something.
I push my hair back, try to think.
The pool lights snap off suddenly
like a cigarette flicked into a lake.

Strong, Dead.

The turning point is invisible
needs drop like spiders to the ground
and glide away as they should.
You won't need a fork anymore.
Conversation dies only once
after you flash
like a burnt lightbulb.
People turn and look
ice clicking in their glasses.
There is something to be learned
but you can't remember what
so you wear a sequined dress to the car
and ride out to see the desert.
Sheep try to beg for food
but move back when you step forward
like a walking x-ray.
In their little heads
the sun on your face
reminds them of something.
Your open mouth looks like home.

Behind Glass

I stand and look at the
Emperor Penguin
imagine the wood frame
a sculpture under skin.

If it falls over
rolls out of the case
ladies will scream
lock themselves in the bathroom.

In the gift shop
a boy digs through hats
finds the right one
wears it out to the hall.
Seven security guards
discuss someone's wife
as the boy slides by.

On Tuesday a car
came through the front door.
The skid marks end
where the teller stands
smiling down on me
as I dig for change.

"You've got enough there,"
she says, and bends
to pull a $50 from my ear.
"Where'd you learn that?"
I ask but she ignores me
smiles, reaches far
down my blouse.
"Where'd you learn that?"
I say dreamily.

Primitive

One tanned arm.

At night the road sweats.
Each restaurant
riddled with light.
I can't smell anything now
no sound in the dark halls
and I wake up
kicking sheets to the floor.

My mother always said
never forget where
you come from.
I drive deeper into
the hopeful quiet.
I do my best.

These hills grow dark
the air shines.
Any hopes I once had
turn off.
Imagine that relief.

Listen for them, the babies
the bombs in the ground
shining under your car
as you pass.
Soon you won't hear
yourself thinking.

How could this be wrong?
Each mistake
all my bad dreams
crushed between my teeth.

I feel a state-line,
a cobweb, float by.

Her Apartment, Her Boyfriend

There's a man standing
on his own lawn
looking up
thinking about Armstrong
walking on the moon.
He waters the grass
hums a song.

Armstrong himself
drinks a glass of beer.
It tastes good to him.

A woman across the way
throws a man out her window.
He lands
does not move.

The Neon Cross

Young boys take turns
being tied up.
Only one seems to enjoy it.
You watch from your car
then take your shirt off
struggle with your pants
and let the snow fall over you.

At times you wish
palm trees would grow here.
You choose movies
set in hot places
and go home without your coat.
The neon cross on the hill
has one arm burnt out.
Boys jump the fence
and draw straws in a huddle.
You run towards them
but the loser is already
badly cut.
He looks up at the cross
and sighs, looks away.

You check into a motel
on the outskirts.
Children hide outside
by the pop machine.
You know they have keys.
You take out your knife
and cut your initials
in the shower curtain
just in case.
For a second it seems too quiet.
You pace before the mirror.
When they cut the tree down
it crushes your car and

the power goes out all over.
You take your shirt off
use it as a fan in the dark.

Gentlemen Take Polaroids

Imagine me
hung out to dry
crying honey
don't leave me this way.

Black Dahlia

Hollywood palm trees lean south
their baffled heads
full of spiders.

Black men audition for roles
as Chinese women.
They clear their throats all day.

Someone has thrown a mannequin
out a car window
the top half here
the bottom half there
its mouth full of dirt.

Someone went by in
a long sedan
a small sports coupe
his hand out the window
his face in darkness.
He sang as he went by.
A child waved
a child on her way home
later changed her mind
said she never did.

In Hollywood every hotel
has a detective.
Every car has bench seats
every mansion weighs a ton.
After a rain, spiders shine
drop from the trees.

A cruiser floats by
the famous lot
their two faces looking

at long grass, garbage
the shape of her body
still there days later.
They turn a corner
watch bungalows roll by.

Chalk Wave
- for Huey P. Long

The last thing he looked up to:
the assembly of men
staring him down.

He walked down the fire escape
minutes before it broke.
Schoolchildren coming down
like hail, denting cars.
The city paved it over
but no one walks there.
They cross the street.

He sees men from behind
their long backs.
He rubs his jaw
and shudders.

When he was young
he closed his eyes
and guessed the shapes:
a square
a triangle
three wavy lines
and every time he was right.

When he was young
he heard things at night
his own voice as an adult
his own slow sigh.

Down south the trees bend low
heavy with moss.
He looks at them with disgust
sees lungs, organs
corrupted by ignorance.

He suspects salvation comes
through women
but keeps it to himself.
Too drunk to move on her bed
he whispers:
take me home take me home
and she covers his mouth
with her long lips.

When the children came down
he knew why

The shots:
a piano passed through
his lung
a lawn mower
through his thigh
several small plates
opened his forehead.
All take him from behind.

When the children came down
he could taste it.

Rural Splendour

A hog shifts a dimpled thigh
groans at all the fences.
The highway, boiled by the sun
moves around the corner
strolls into the trees
forgetting to cover its trail.
There are no mice in the fields
just wheat bone dry
the sun floating down.

The sun has experience
and no imagination.
What it sees, it knows.
Nothing can escape itself.
Imagine a blade of grass
growing in your skin, imagine
the grass drying to paper in your flesh.
Now imagine the moon
which has no facts and knows nothing.
Your skin half finished
rising out of the black.
You are no different from the fields
the fences. You walk into the trees
and are gone.
The man that follows you
is pulling an apple cart.

Some Left in the Bowl

The dog slinks in
looks at the baby.
Steps forward over plastic toys.

A tea kettle hisses
my father is missing
his safety rope still hanging
from the roof he was shingling.

A pot boils over.
My mother's cigarette burns down
drops off to the carpet.
The house goes up in seconds.

With all the doors open
the house stands in a cool breeze
and the dog trots out the back.
I put my mother's cigarette
between my lips
and carry on like her.

The Pressures in His Pocket

I'm seventeen
tearing up the grass
to get to the car.
Oil pan, V-6, one soft one
the road out of here
one soft one.
stop.
will be home soon
stop.

Remarkable Organ

We go to funerals
and wait.
Blah blah blah organ music.
He never forgets his wallet.

He's sitting there
looking at me
his legs apart
and I try to look away.
How do I tell him
there is a hole in my apartment.
I put a chair down there
it came back up smaller.

I Don't Feel Like Stopping Yet

Open your arms to me
take me through your doors
one more time.
I'll do it til I get it right.
I'll bend down kiss the
cigarette burns, eat the streamers
I'll follow you
down alleys, lie in dumpsters
and look up at the studded sky
in adoration.
Just don't say I lost it all.

Take pictures of me
on the strip at night.
I will visit my room
empty the suitcase
like an archeologist.
I will pull out my own skull.

Let circus-circus be there
above me like a halo
because I am purified by night
by the smoke in lounges.
Searching me out like the snake
it comes to say: open your hand
and be God.
I have a new way of counting.
I give each machine a name.

My father's shoes were stolen
on a train in Berlin.

He walked in stocking feet.
He stood by fountains and stared.
Sitting on the back
of a stone lion he waved
as the trucks went by.
He waited for the streetlights.

The clouds in Berlin hang low
the walls of buildings are black.
My father put one foot behind the other
and stepped into his bright future.

Fly Paper

I'm going to find him
though he threw his teeth
back into the burning house
watched each explode
like popcorn.

I see his car crossing
the Hoover Dam
crawling the red hills
and his cigarette butts
dropped behind
so he can get back.

Somewhere he turns a corner
eyes a waitress.
Somewhere he coughs long and sharp
and veins stick out
so he knows he's not dead.
Or maybe he signed his name
lost his wallet
touched something he shouldn't.
The closer I get
the more his hand will falter.

Monday Went Out

There is a blackened end of stick
in my throat rotting me
from up to down
and I wait for you
the three o'clock moment
when you rise up
and come at me
hands open to the crust.

Monday slid by on grease
and left me here with you
sick in my bathing cap
and trunks.

What do I expect from you
that's the question?
Perhaps a hesitation.
A funny look when you say
goodbye
a threat I can take
home with me
and eat.

Heavin' Tots

She loves this part of herself.
The tiny bubbles, the tiny coats
and that sloshing sound
everywhere she goes.

30 She wades into the long grass
sets them down under
a hot moon in a black sky.
They struggle but only go in circles.

When she places the first
in the slingshot its arms wave
like weeds under water.
They snap into the world, one by one.

Maps

What you say
gives me the urge
to anchor here
my legs trembling
to close my eyes
and see the rivers
the red and blue
highways snap back up
into the tape-measure.

I know what's out there:
a thousand rabbits
thrown into the ditch.

Something squirms under
your new shirt.
You smile
wipe a drop of sweat away.

His Encore Even Better

Any man with a face like that
will be the baby of all eyes
will die of fame.

The cross-eyed boulevards curve
to accommodate his one short leg
distorted gardens spring up behind.
There are kites, dogs roll over
and I watch him through the streamers
the topsoil shaking from his pantleg
and his gentle confused step.
The cement cracks, we go blind looking.
This man has us, and we drop
into his capable palm like seeds.

Intercourse

I am sorry my car is
pillaging your house
your dog burned raw
under the roaring wheels.
I am sorry I have taken
your husband
bitten him hard
so he had to confess
the mark shaped like
an eyelash.

I watch you go
through the hedges
looking for your gun
and I feel pity
as you turn over
each rotten leaf.

But you should know
I did it for you
ate that uranium
and grew
took things from banks
and slept singing
in the freight elevator
so I could catch a glimpse
of you
pulling the red silk
from your mouth
taking the turban
from your glorious head
and giving it to him.
That's why I took him
because he has everything.

She had very pretty legs
but could not stand on them
or look at them for long.
Summer seemed to slow down
then reverse.
Her uncles left, then came back
then walked backwards
out of her life.

She used to get drunk
on Mother's brandy.
Life was one damned
fruit cocktail after another
one poached salmon
one crisp white bed
one chaise longue on the grass.
She sat by the woods
watching the sky sink.

She turned thirty.
The summer sped backwards
and backflipped into winter.
She grew a white hair
to keep occupied.
Sometimes she would say
she had someone else's legs.

She told long stories
after dinner.
Her uncles would laugh
slap their heavy thighs
but after dinner
wake with a jolt
dreaming she is near.

Wet Redhead

The moment before waking
that sharp truncated scream
lost in her passing out.
That's what I eat, wake to
have with me on the bus.

At night I hear
a dragging foot go by.
The cars don't make it
up the hill.
Is my window open?

Where she rises
the clot of earth
the wet still there.
I breath her in
tell her about work.
I am sorry now
try to be her friend.
She is in my shoes.
I put them on her
working the foot in.

But she grew
opened her mouth
and spoke.

She
my wallpaper
the noises I hear at night
slipping under my sheets
making each hair
stand up cold.
I smell her.
When I come home
I know she has
searched my room.

Tangential Advice

In Utah if you leave your car
lizards climb in and drive off.
They heap their bodies
on the accelerator.
They hang from the wheel.

A long Ford screams down the I-90
until stopped by something big.
Red hills slide over windows.

If you jingle your keys
a thousand tiny eyes shift.
If you smile at your wife
their uneven fingers itch.
They want to crawl into your clothes
and walk down the main street
a dufflebag full of fingers.
They congregate at night
outside your hotel room.
They add themselves together
and come up with you.

Miami

Sand and sea.
A rosette of avenues
and gardened overpasses.
This open and shut
motel lobby
and pink wallpaper in each room
reminding us of our childhood.

Under the boardwalk
a hundred little ladies
full of tequila
are relieved of their winnings.

A Bed on a Barge, Raining

I dip my feet in the sink
begin to shave my legs
A fish burps from the drain
then insects surge up.

Kevin thinks I do not
tidy often enough.
My friends don't drop by.
My mother cries into the phone.

I read that short story guy
and cry to myself.
When Kevin comes home
I feel depressed.
He looks at all the fish
looks at me.
He knows I am losing this one.

A Job For the Skunk Police

The block I live on
changed directions today.
Dad fell out of bed.

The boys meet at the fort
and wait for me
so I can prick their
fingers, collect the blood.

I shake sometimes
holding the pin.

If it weren't for
the skunk police
the backyard would be empty.
But they dig up the rhubarb
knock through the hedges
shouting "here pussy!"

I pace, wondering where the boys went.
I look down my own pants.

Insomnia

I had nothing left to give
the door was closed
and he waited there.
But my feet were ruined
all that glass.

I could only wait for him
lie on the table
no gun, no muscle
my white skin smoldering
his voice over the p.a.
"you're making this too easy."

When Ted Lavinder Was Shot

I had a baby then
in my pocket.

It was like Dallas:
me in every camera
two, three places
at the same moment
all over town.

People remembered seeing me
talking to me
years later
where I hadn't been.

There are books
with colour inserts
and as I say
I had this baby
and the problem was
where to keep it.
I wouldn't want a mistake.
I wouldn't want
those red and white banners
floating down to us all
in the parade grounds
like disappointments
candy gone hard.

How do you know when his
mouth is open?
How can you be sure it
will stay that way
so you can put it in there?
That was my question
as a plane went over

the band blared as he rose
to take the podium.
The baby kacked loudly
and someone looked over.
That's when I took the safety off
and started firing.

Two Grunts in the Sea

But there is no water
even in the taps
I lie on the bed
in a slip, my legs apart
waiting for night.

Sun floods the blinds
as he lies beside me
his chest higher than mine.
I sit up and check
he is bigger than I am.

At night the streetlamps
pour over us
I turn over, sigh.

Water battering a car
the door too heavy to open
my own face in the window
speaking, but I want to stop.
I sit up to motel room
my stomach sweating and round.

He has a voice in the bathroom.
Sings and holds his beer.
He comes out singing.

You're awake, he whispers
and comes to lie there
to spread himself over me.
What's that noise he says
what's that roaring?
The ceiling breaks up
the whole outside bursts in.

Suppose you had a mouthfull of corn flakes.
Suppose you had a red sox shirt
and woke to a perfect American morning
the airports clear
the cereal bowls ready
the fires blazing at night on tv.
Suppose I took a whip to your dog
and ate all your grass
or bought a goat
a foreign goat
to eat all your grass and kick
your trash can down the street.
If your drain burped insects
and every morning the street blew up.
In the deep black of night
trapped under your tight covers
dreaming of the sound of music
and the interlude won't end
how could you keep the hat on your head?
If you turned around on a weekend
the lawns burning orange
and saw me standing there
how could you give up on me?

"Ring Bell For Service"

These are the hotel rooms
the lounge, the damp offices.
An ape waits
at reception
holding his breath.
He has simple needs
and they are not being met.

Hot air sighs from
the elevator doors.
The ice machine overflows
and our friend looks guilty
rubbing his small head.
Something says: leave now.

Weeks later he sends
a telegram
HAVE LOST EVERYTHING
AM COMING HOME
he steps from the lobby
smaller than
when he went in.

The sun falls on him
throws him to the ground
ravaging his fur
seeking out the soft
white places
where an ape
hurts most.

I Never Had Enough

Wild and flooded forehead
and fingers thick with sadness
we touched each other
looked over the edge to 5th ave
saw office windows descend
get smaller.

This is the life.
Getting smaller as we go down
our clothes like a fashion-shoot
and me smiling into you
smiling over the edge
of a shrunken life.

You wouldn't like this
if you were my last man.
You'd say:
where does all this lead?

Religious Carpool

It started with James.
Then Jeannie.
I felt it slip beneath
my upper lip on Wednesday.
We sing sometimes
and sometimes it feels good.
I pick James up
then Jeannie picks me up.
We sing again
looking for the station
and when the poppies go by
we fall asleep at the wheel
our three mouths open
and our arms spread wide.
Afterwards we compare
who caught the most broken glass.
They sting us like bees
and I save things in jars:
glass, teeth
weeds from ditches we go into.
I keep relics.
I have my own finger.

An Opening

"To get out of this Pope suit"
I tell the personnel officer.
She has been asking about
my goals and objectives.

At a certain point
there is a change in the air.
I breathe in its scent
lean back in my chair.

"Personally," I tell her
"I would prefer to own everything.
in *me* is pure aggressive right.
You can feel it, can't you?"

She has small eyes
and looks out the window
to other buildings.
Her pen bounces on the desk
she bites her lip.
I can tell she has married
the wrong man
she is beginning to sense it.

I lean forward
I turn on the highbeams.
"You have something that hurts"
I murmur
"Secrets of the flesh
questions
you stay awake long after it's over
don't you?"
It all goes as before.
She smiles weakly and signs
her form where I tell her.

Rousseau

He sits on Hume's knee
the trite red mouth
in a French pout: mon ami
he giggles
every fold in his pile of tires
ajiggle.
Mon ami
get a woman for God's sake
you are no fun anymore.
Come to Tahiti
where the girls grow suddenly
and they will all be afraid
of your ridiculous beard.
Mon homme
he tickles the granite chin
get laid once before you die.

The True Name

I eat nails to show
that I am sorry
I bend double
try to walk
soon I find
I crave the wrong things
my hands turn backwards.

I wait to be told
it doesn't work
I wait to be shown
your back.

He drives past the Christmas trees
his mouth open.
Perhaps he is trying to cry.
Baubles float in the air.
He could reach out and take one
but there is no lanky blonde
to give them to.
In fact no one
puts her heels on his shoulders.
No one whispers "make me."

He stands at the window
steps out onto the roof.
Neighbouring dogs
shake their chains, cough.
He lets these dress pants
fall to his feet in the snow.
Baubles, bells float by.
His eyes close
then he lets go a flood
of shadow and light
which floats down in ribbons.
Children rush
to the head of the stairs and yell
"He's lonely again!"

What Have You Done With Your Gardener?

So many holes
so little in the way
of shovels.

We have done
questionable things
and we would like
to talk to you.
Could you listen
at night
when dinner is
finished
when we are drunk on wine?

It was a silly fear we had
an idea crept up at night
and we sat and watched
his hunched form
pulling the weeds.
It felt like every
vein we had.

We have walked
out over the grass
into the lake
and thought about the bottom
like a floor, like
there is a wheelbarrow meant
to nose down that incline.

I let him take me.
I'll admit that.
I rolled over and
watched the rocks.

We don't mean anybody harm.
We have our own lives

and ideas.
See, here are
rose bushes weighing
thirty pounds each
that grow and grow.
We hear noises
down in there.

Speed Creates Pure Objects

No, I can't taste anything
just the radio.

I believe these are signals:
something trotting along
just out of sight
raising dust;
a hole in the back seat;
my new haircut.

I roll by on four drums
hounding the red hills
boring holes where Vegas
used to be.